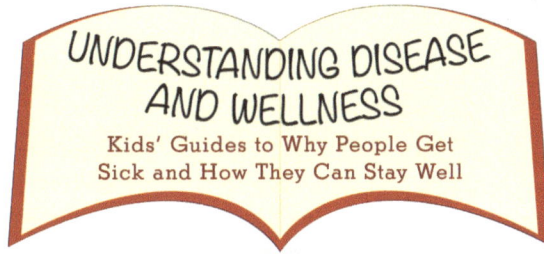

UNDERSTANDING DISEASE AND WELLNESS

Kids' Guides to Why People Get
Sick and How They Can Stay Well

A KID'S GUIDE TO
BUGS
AND HOW THEY CAN
MAKE YOU SICK

VILLAGE EARTH PRESS

Series List

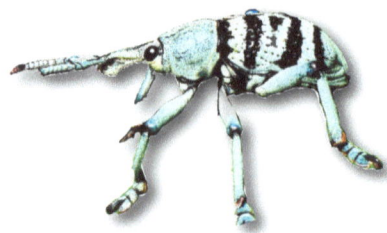

UNDERSTANDING DISEASE AND WELLNESS

Kids' Guides to Why People Get Sick and How They Can Stay Well

A KID'S GUIDE TO BUGS
AND HOW THEY CAN MAKE YOU SICK

Rae Simons

Understanding Disease and Wellness:
Kids' Guides to Why People Get Sick and How They Can Stay Well
A KID'S GUIDE TO BUGS AND HOW THEY CAN MAKE YOU SICK

Village Earth Press
Vestal, New York 13850
www.villageearthpress.com

First Printing
9 8 7 6 5 4 3 2 1

Series ISBN (paperback): 978-1-62524-445-1
ISBN (paperback): 978-1-62524-419-2
ebook ISBN: 978-1-62524-054-5

Library of Congress Control Number: 2013911247

Author: Simons, Rae

Note: This book is a revised and updated edition of *Bugs Can Make You Sick!* (ISBN: 978-1-934970-12-6), published in 2009 by Alpha House Publishing.

Introduction

According to a recent study reported in the Virginia Henderson International Nursing Library, kids worry about getting sick. They worry about AIDS and cancer, about allergies and the "super-germs" that resist medication. They know about these ills—but they don't always understand what causes them or how they can be prevented.

Unfortunately, most 9- to 11-year-olds, the study found, get their information about diseases like AIDS from friends and television; only 20 percent of the children interviewed based their understanding of illness on facts they had learned at school. Too often, kids believe urban legends, schoolyard folktales, and exaggerated movie plots. Oftentimes, misinformation like this only makes their worries worse. The January 2008 *Child Health News* reported that 55 percent of all children between 9 and 13 "worry almost all the time" about illness.

This series, **Understanding Disease and Wellness**, offers readers clear information on various illnesses and conditions, as well as the immunizations that can prevent many diseases. The books dispel the myths with clearly presented facts and colorful, accurate illustrations. Better yet, these books will help kids understand not only illness—but also what they can do to stay as healthy as possible.

—*Dr. Elise Berlan*

Just the Facts

- Although most bugs are harmless, some can bite, sting, or even spread disease.

- Ticks can spread many different diseases.

- Mosquitoes carry malaria, especially in hot parts of the world.

- West Nile disease is carried by birds and spread to humans by mosquitoes. This sickness can cause fever, headache, and confusion.

- Flies carry diseases like dysentery or pink eye, which can be spread to people when flies walk on food.

- Some insects are poisonous and their bite or sting can be dangerous. These include scorpions and some spiders and ants.

- For people who are allergic to bug bites or bee stings, being bitten can be life-threatening.

- Going to the doctor is a good way to prevent the kinds of sicknesses bugs spread.

- You can protect yourself against insects by using repellent or covering your skin.

- Scientists are always doing more research so that people can stay safe from disease and understand insects better.

Scary Bugs

Lots of people don't like *bugs*. Plenty of bugs are helpful and harmless, though, no matter how scary they may look. Many insects and other bug-like creatures eat other pests or help the environment in other ways.

The bugs shown on these pages may look dangerous, but these beetles are examples of insects that are harmless to human beings.

Words to Know

Bugs: when people use this word, they usually mean insects (creatures with six legs), spiders (which have eight legs), or centipedes or millipedes (which have many legs).

Really Scary Bugs

Although most bugs are harmless, some bugs really are dangerous. Some bugs—like spiders, bees, and mosquitoes—can bite or sting you, leaving behind a little bit of poison. People who are *allergic* to this poison can have very serious, even *life-threatening* reactions to bug bites and stings. For most of us, though, these bites and stings will leave behind only an itchy or sore bump. A few bugs, especially certain kinds of spiders, have very poisonous bites that need to be treated by a doctor immediately.

But the biggest and scariest problem with bugs is that some of them, especially mosquitoes and flies, can spread diseases. Some of these illnesses aren't very serious—but others are deadly. Diseases that are spread by insects are big problems around the world.

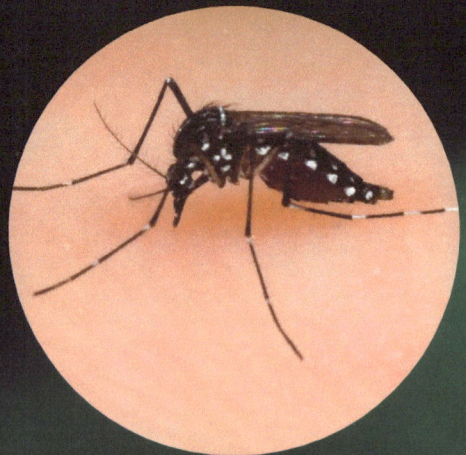

Allergic: very sensitive to certain substances, to the point that a person may become very sick.

Life-threatening: having the ability to kill.

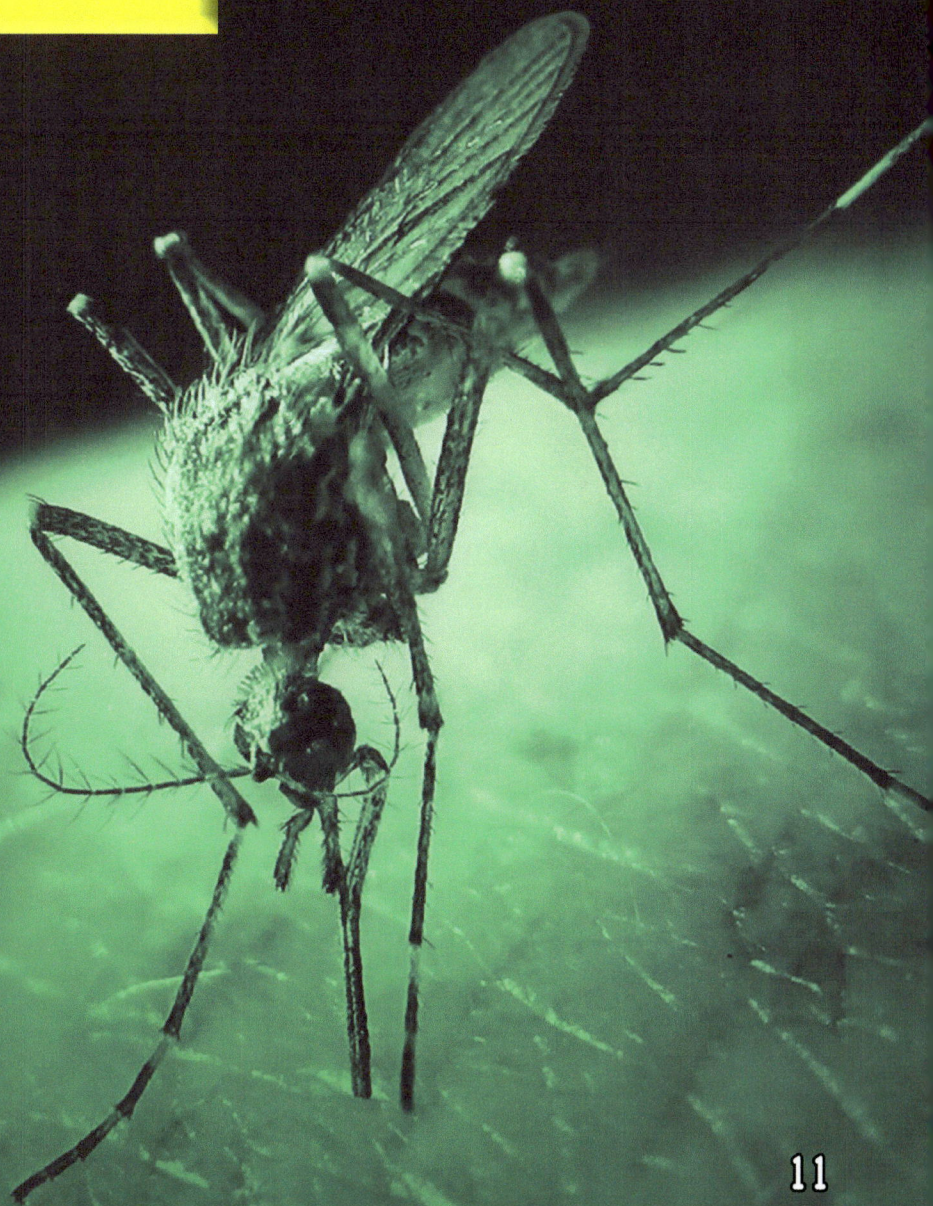

Lyme Disease

Not all ticks cause Lyme disease. The tick shown on this page is called a lone star tick, and it does not carry Lyme disease. Its bite may make you a little itchy, but it won't make you sick. The tick on the next page, though, is the type that lives on deer. If you're walking in the woods or through tall grass, you could pick up one of these disease-carrying creatures.

One of the diseases spread by a bug is Lyme disease, which is carried by deer ticks. The bacteria that causes the disease gets into people if they are bit by this tick.

Antibiotics: medicines used to treat infections and diseases caused by bacteria (tiny, one-celled creatures).

Lyme disease can cause a rash and sore joints. The disease lasts a long time, but it can be treated with *antibiotics*.

When walking in areas where there may be deer ticks, wear long pants and socks. When you're back home, check yourself for any ticks and remove them immediately.

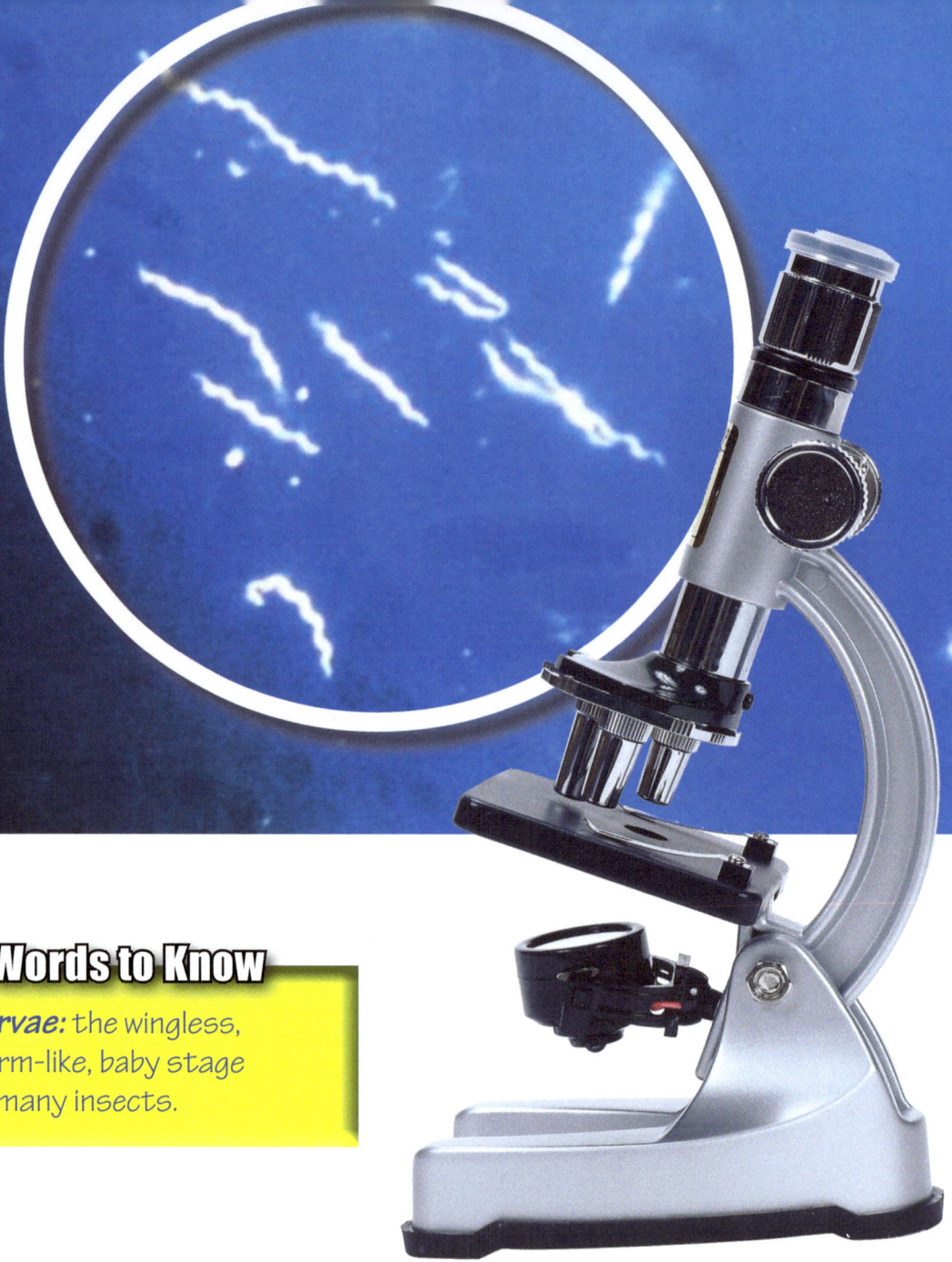

If you were to look through a microscope at the tiny creatures that cause Lyme disease, this is what you would see. These bacteria live on mice, squirrels, and other small animals. Tick *larvae* take the bacteria into their bodies when they feed on these animals' blood.

When the adult tick bites a larger animal—like a human being!—it passes the bacteria into the bloodstream of that animal.

One of the first symptoms of Lyme disease is a "bulls-eye" rash like the one shown here. Go to the doctor immediately if you find a rash like this on yourself.

Malaria

Malaria is a very serious disease that can sometimes be *fatal*. It causes fever, chills, and flu-like symptoms. Mosquitoes that live in certain parts of the world spread this disease to humans.

Words to Know

Fatal: causing death.

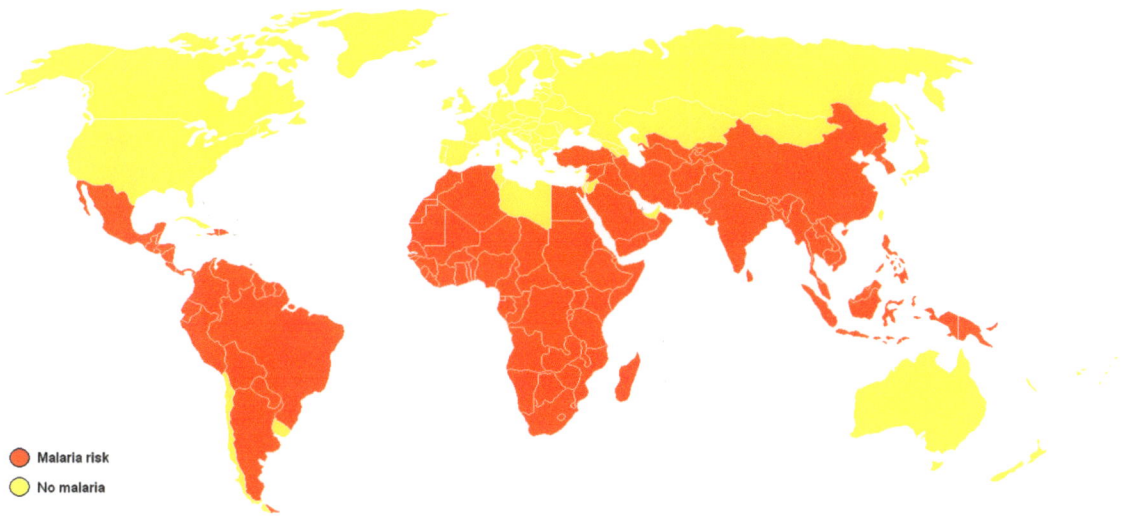

Malaria risk
No malaria

The red areas on this map show where malaria is common. Between 300 and 500 million people get malaria every year. More than a million of them die. The disease is an especially big problem in the world's poorer countries, where good medical care is not available. When so many people are getting sick, it makes these countries become even poorer. So this is a very big problem caused by a very small bug!

This illustration shows a mosquito drinking its blood meal. When it does, it passes along the tiny *parasite* that causes malaria. The parasite then passes into the human's *liver*.

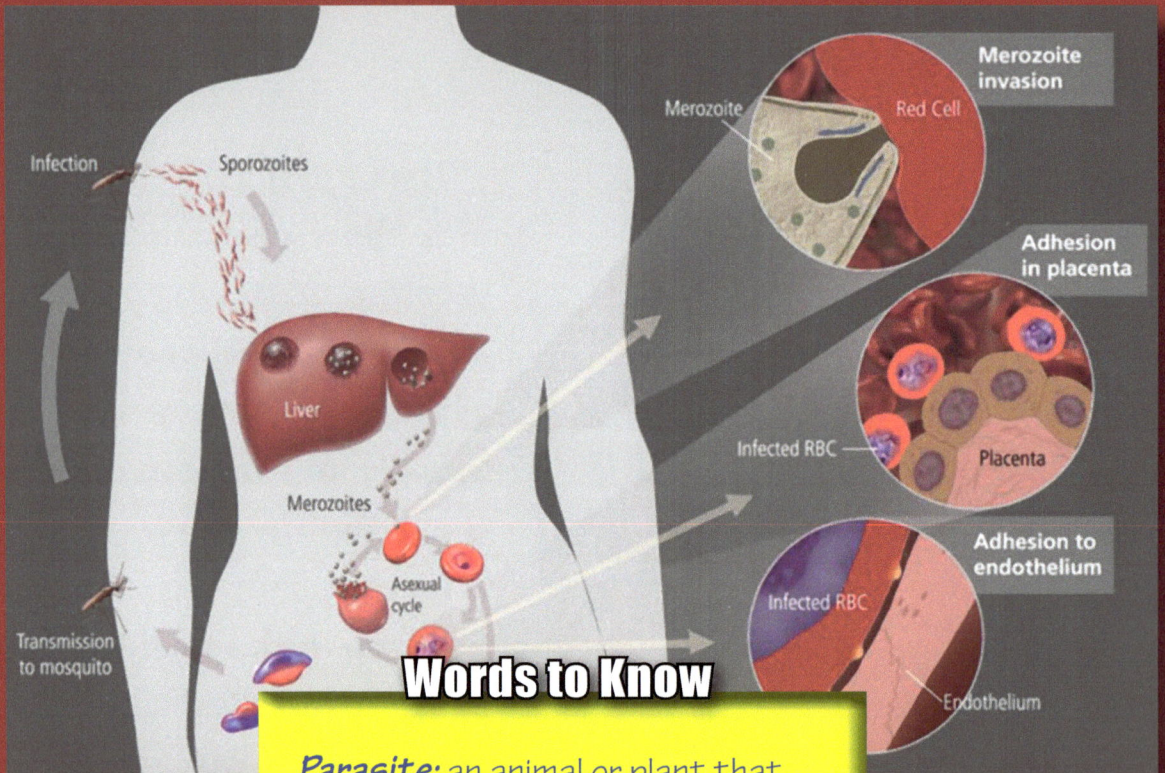

Infection

Sporozoites

Liver

Merozoites

Asexual cycle

Transmission to mosquito

Merozoite invasion

Merozoite

Red Cell

Adhesion in placenta

Infected RBC

Placenta

Adhesion to endothelium

Infected RBC

Endothelium

Words to Know

Parasite: an animal or plant that lives in or on a host (another animal or plant) and gets its nourishment (food) from the host without giving anything to the host in return.

Liver: a large organ (shown above) that helps with digestion. It also helps remove harmful substances from your body. If your liver can't do its job, you will get very sick.

If you've been infected with malaria, you'll usually start feeling sick about two to four weeks later. You might, however, not begin to feel ill until as much as a year later.

If you don't normally live in an area where malaria is common but you plan to travel to one of these regions, a doctor can give you medicine that will help protect you against this disease. If you think you might have been exposed to malaria, see a doctor. She will look for the parasite in a drop of your blood under a microscope. There are medicines that can cure malaria, and it is important to begin taking them as soon as possible.

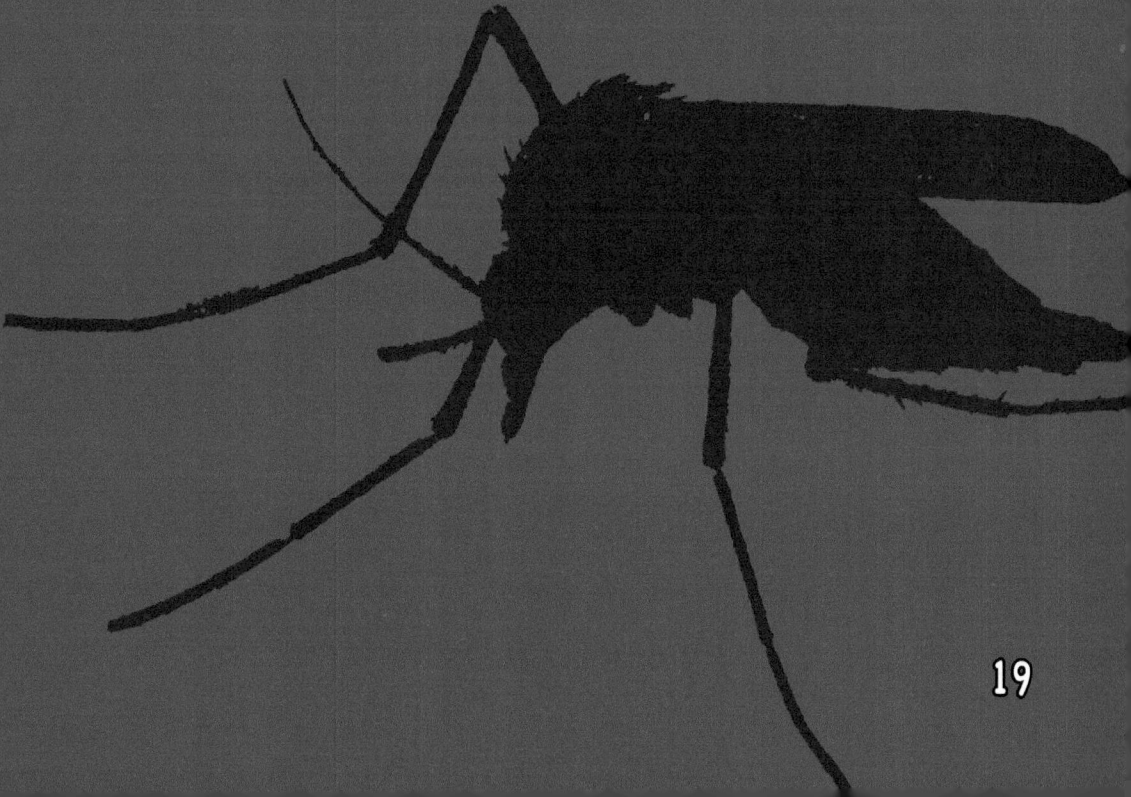

West Nile Disease

West Nile disease is carried by mosquitoes in Africa, Asia, Europe, and North America. The *virus* (shown magnified many thousands of times at right) is carried on birds, which then pass it on to humans through mosquitoes.

Many people who get this disease have very mild symptoms. Some people may not even know they are sick. Most people will get better without any medical treatment. In a few cases, however, people with West Nile disease can become seriously ill. They will have a high fever, stiff neck, severe headache, and *disorientation*.

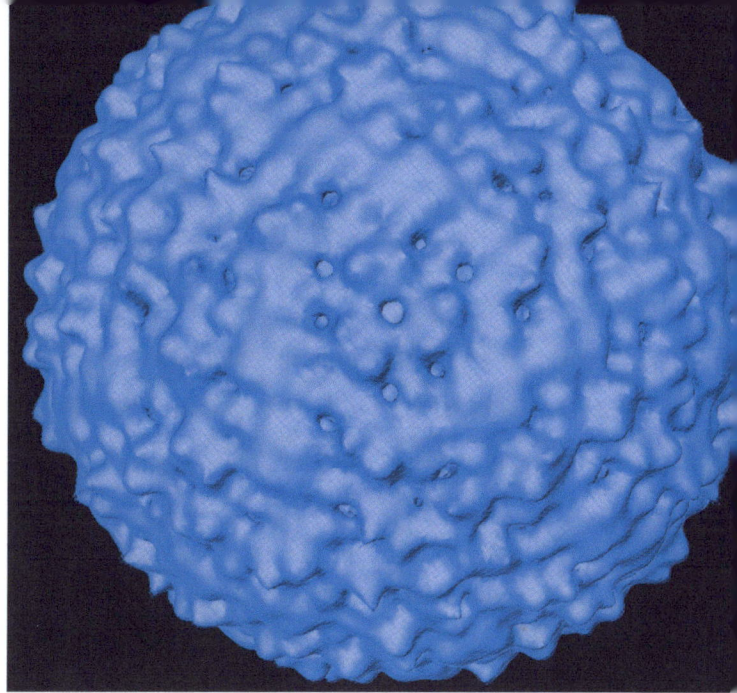

Words to Know

Virus: a very tiny organism that needs to invade a living cell in order to grow.

Disorientation: mental confusion.

ASK THE DOCTOR

West Nile disease is scary. What can I do to keep from getting it?

A: First of all, remember that most cases of West Nile virus are mild and people get better all by themselves. Next, take these steps to protect yourself: Use insect repellent. Wear long-sleeved shirts and pants when possible. Get rid of mosquito-breeding sites by emptying standing water from any containers around your home. Stay indoors between dusk and dawn, when mosquitoes are most active. Use screens on windows to keep mosquitoes out. And if you find a dead bird, don't handle it.

WHAT HAPPENS ON THE INSIDE?

Serious cases of West Nile virus cause mental confusion and even *coma*. This happens on the **outside**. Meanwhile, *inside*, the brain becomes inflamed. This means the tissue becomes swollen in response to the infection.

Older people are most at risk of developing a serious case of West Nile disease. Scientists have not yet found a cure for this disease, so the best approach is to avoid contact with mosquitoes that may spread the virus.

Words to Know

Coma: a state of sleep-like unconsciousness that can last for hours, days, or even years.

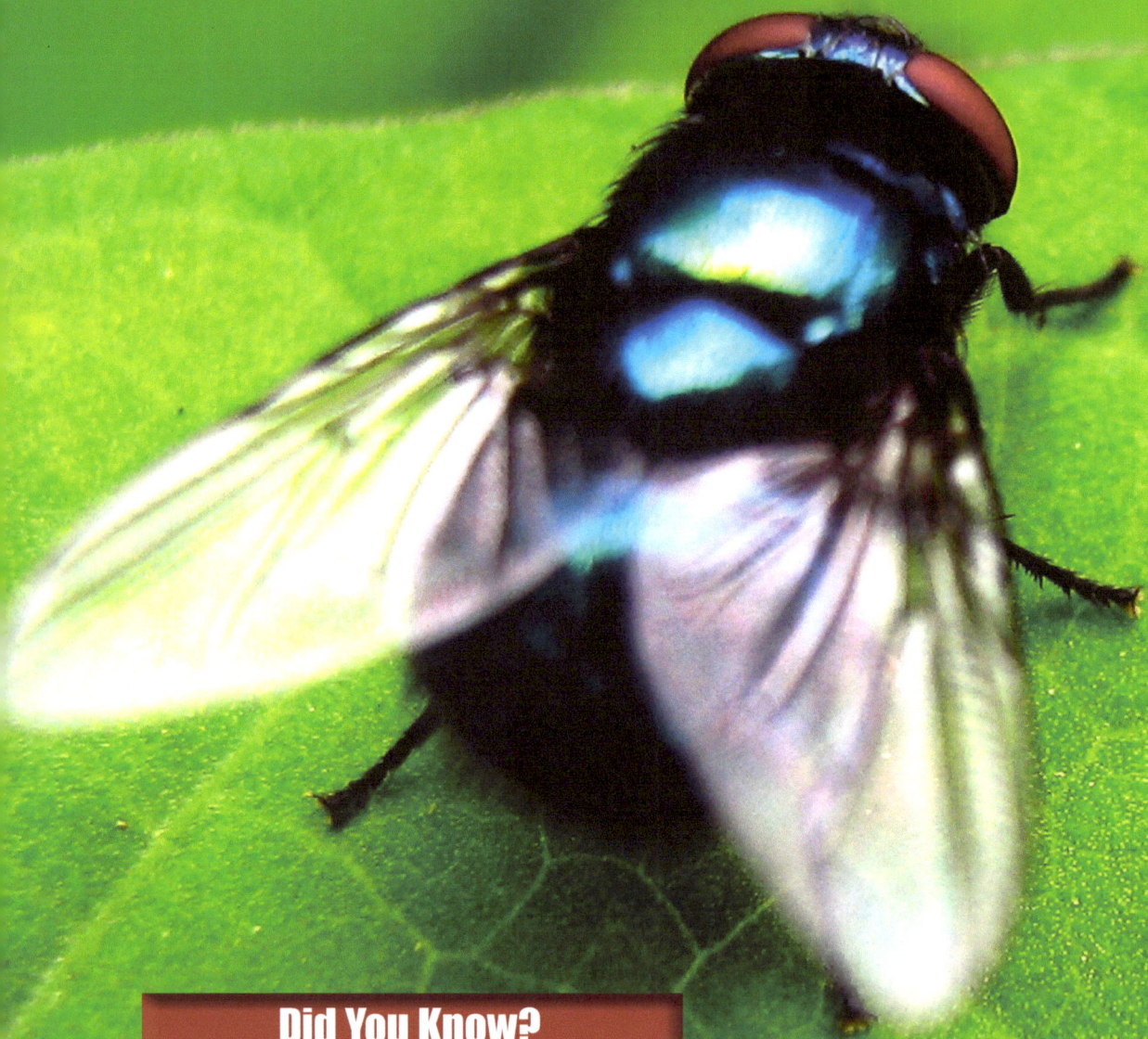

Flies

Did You Know?

Flies have really dirty feet! After walking on so much excrement, flies may carry as many as 6 million bacteria on their feet.

Many kinds of bacteria and parasites live on flies. These insects are attracted to places where germs thrive—like *excrement*, rotten food, and dead and decaying animal bodies. This means that when flies crawl on things, their legs and saliva often spread disease.

What can you do to protect yourself? Cover foods to prevent flies from crawling on them. Don't eat food where flies have crawled. If you know a fly has crawled on your skin, wash with soap and water, especially if you have an open sore or scratch. Use screens in open windows, and keep doors shut during warm weather.

Words to Know

Excrement: a polite word for poop or bowel movements.

25

Intestinal: having to do with the intestines, the tubes inside your stomach through which food passes as it is digested.

Flies can spread many different kinds of diseases.

One of these diseases is dysentery, which is caused by a parasite that is sometimes found on uncooked meat. When flies crawl on the meat, they then carry the parasite to humans. Dysentery causes diarrhea and bad stomach cramps.

Flies can also spread other *intestinal* diseases, as well as polio, leprosy, and tuberculosis.

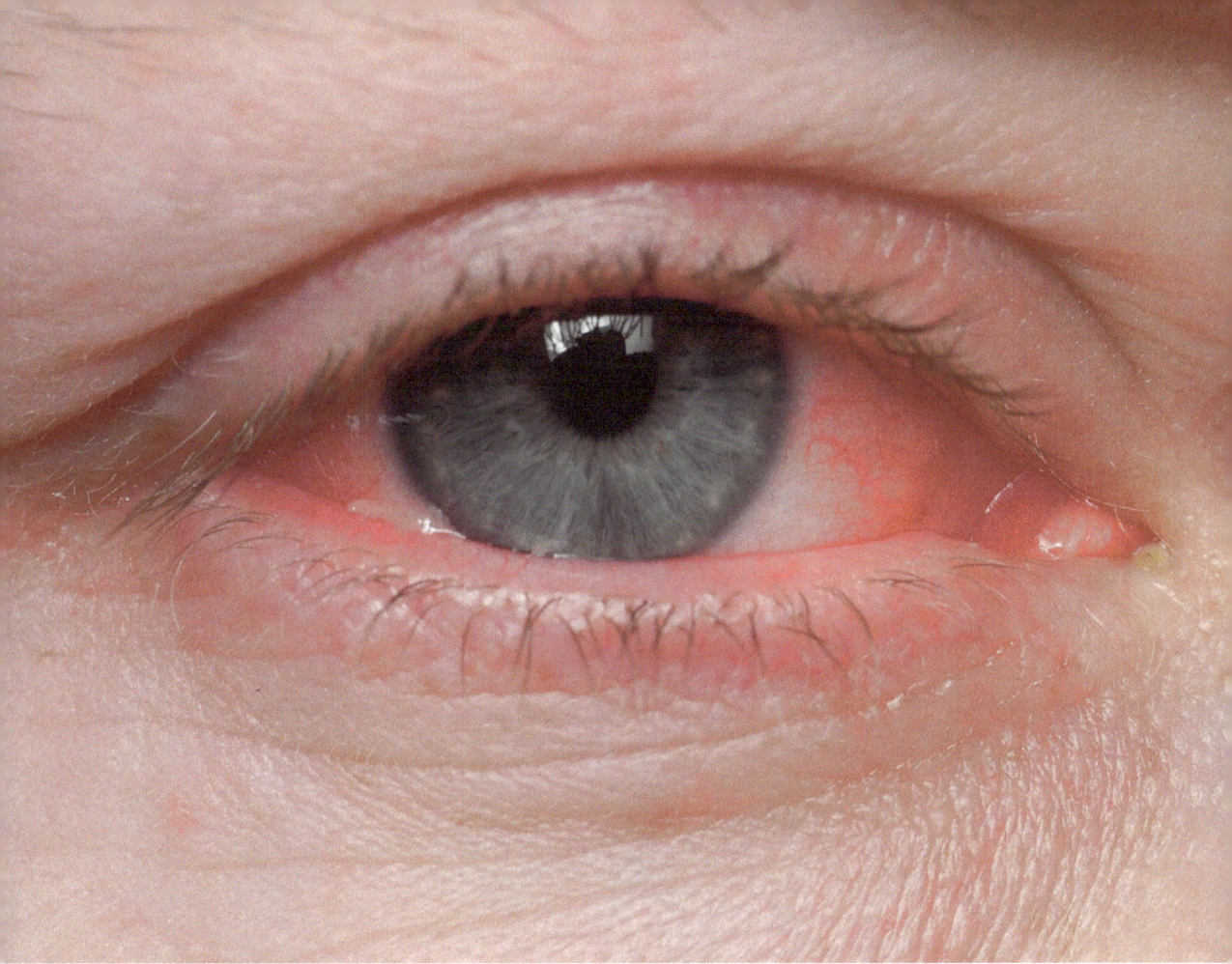

Flies not only have germs sticking to their legs—they also spread their excrement and saliva wherever they crawl. As you can imagine, fly poop and fly spit have plenty of germs! Flies also sometimes lay their eggs in open wounds. So get rid of flies with swatters and sticky traps. And don't leave garbage out for them to crawl on.

Some diseases caused by flies are very serious, while others are merely annoying or painful. Conjuctivitis—pinkeye—is an unpleasant eye condition that can be spread by flies.

Poisonous Bugs

Scorpions are *arachnids* that sting. Some kinds of scorpions cause painful stings that go away by themselves after a couple of hours. Other scorpions are very poisonous. Their bites can be fatal if they're not treated by a doctor. Most of these deadly scorpions are found in Mexico. However, even the less dangerous scorpions can cause serious results if they bite someone who is young or very allergic to the scorpion venom.

The black widow spider is another arachnid that is very poisonous. It is found throughout North America. If a healthy person is bitten by a black widow, he or she will get severe muscle pains and cramps, but most people will recover by themselves. Doctors may give *antivenom* medication to those who are at risk for a more serious reaction.

Words to Know

Arachnids: 8-legged bugs. Ticks are arachnids, as are spiders, scorpions, and mites.

Antivenom: medicine used to treat the venom (poison) of spiders and snakes.

Words to Know

Centipedes: although their name literally means "a hundred feet," these creatures have various numbers of legs—but they always have one pair of legs per body segment.

Centipedes are another kind of bug that sometimes has a poisonous bite. Different kinds of centipedes are found all over the world. Athough their bites can be painful, they're not usually dangerous. Small children or people who are allergic may have more serious reactions.

Ants win first prize for being the most poisonous insects of all. (Not all ants are that poisonous, only certain kinds, such as fire ants and harvester ants.) Some ants sting and others bite. Still others bite and then spray venom on the area they just bit.

Did You Know?

Fire ants release a chemical that tells all the fire ants in the area to sting at the same time. This means it can be really, really painful if you get into a fire ant nest! So stay away from their mounds—and if you do get bit, take an antihistamine, a special medicine that helps reduce allergic reactions.

Allergic Reactions

Getting bitten by a bug isn't pleasant, but it's not usually dangerous. Running into a bug's stinger or bite can be life-threatening, though, if you're allergic. That's true for 5 percent of all people (five out of every hundred).

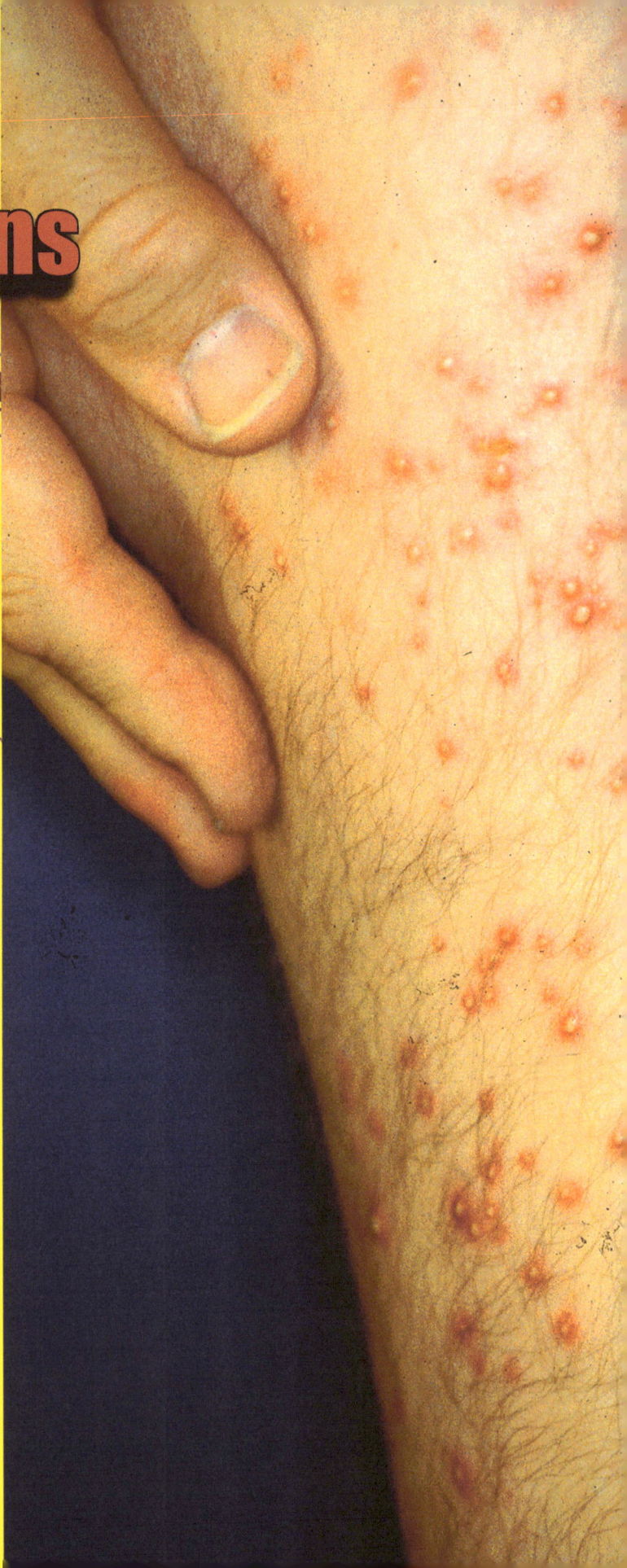

Symptoms of an allergic reaction range from itching and swelling to tightness in the throat and breathing difficulties.

Serious allergic reactions can cause a dangerous drop in blood pressure and unconsciousness. Very serious reactions can stop a person's heart.

Allergic reactions usually occur within minutes of being bitten or stung. Prompt treatment saves lives.

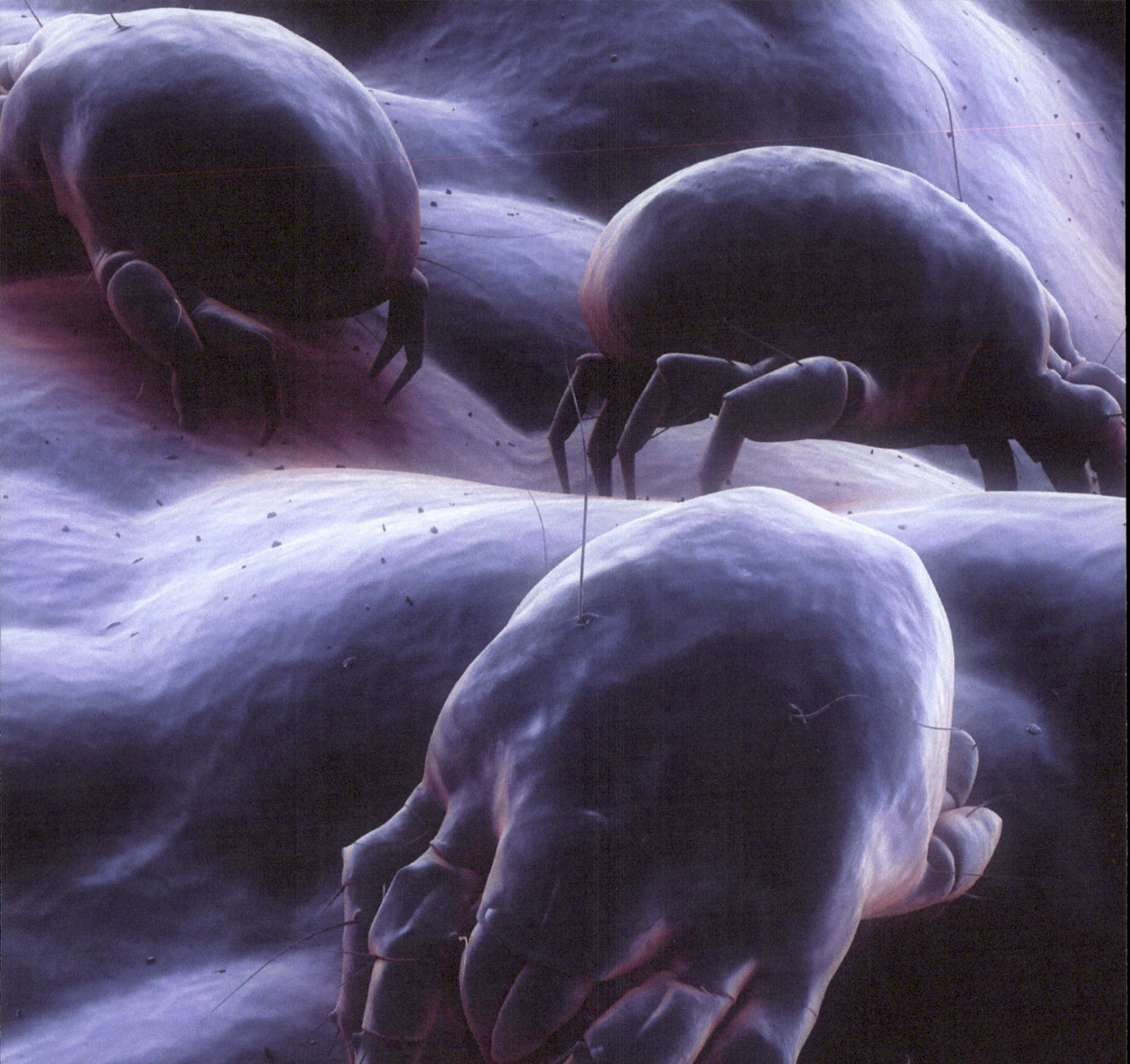

Did You Know?

You could be sharing your bed with anywhere from 100,000 to 10 million dust mites! No matter how creepy this may seem, if you're not allergic, they're harmless. Dust-proof covers for mattresses and pillows cut down on the number of creatures sharing your bed. So does washing bedding regularly.

The most common insect allergy is triggered by tiny creatures you can't even see—dust mites (shown here magnified thousands of times).

These *microscopic* organisms, which are related to spiders, like to live where it's warm and moist—on mattresses, carpets, and furniture, for instance. They eat dead skin cells. They leave behind excrement (poop) and their decaying dead bodies, which then mixes with dust and becomes airborne. If you aren't allergic to it, it's not harmful. But if you are allergic, inhaling this dust can make you sneeze, make your eyes water, and make your nose run. Asthma, a more serious breathing disorder, can also be triggered by dust mites. If you have asthma, your doctor may give you medicine you inhale to help keep open your air passageways.

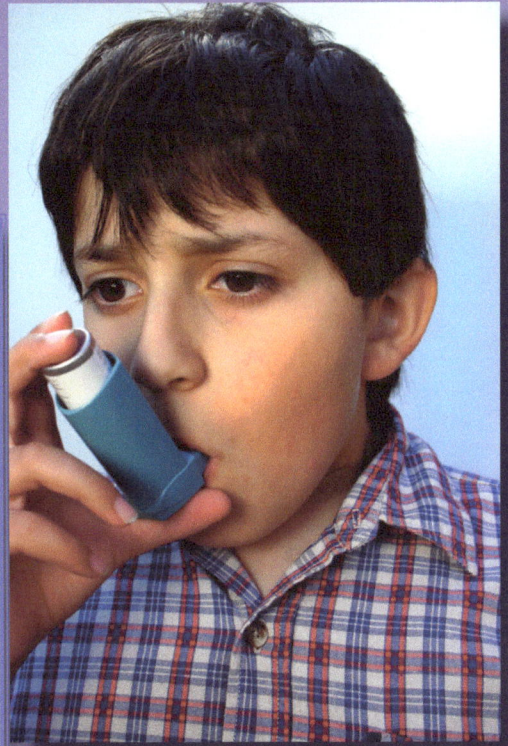

Words to Know

Microscopic: so tiny that it is only visible through a microscope.

Going to the Doctor

There's no reason to spend your life being scared of bugs! Although none of us can completely avoid these creatures, doctors can treat the unpleasant and dangerous conditions insects and other bugs can cause. Doctors have medicines that can prevent or cure many illnesses, and other medicines that can make the *symptoms* less severe or dangerous.

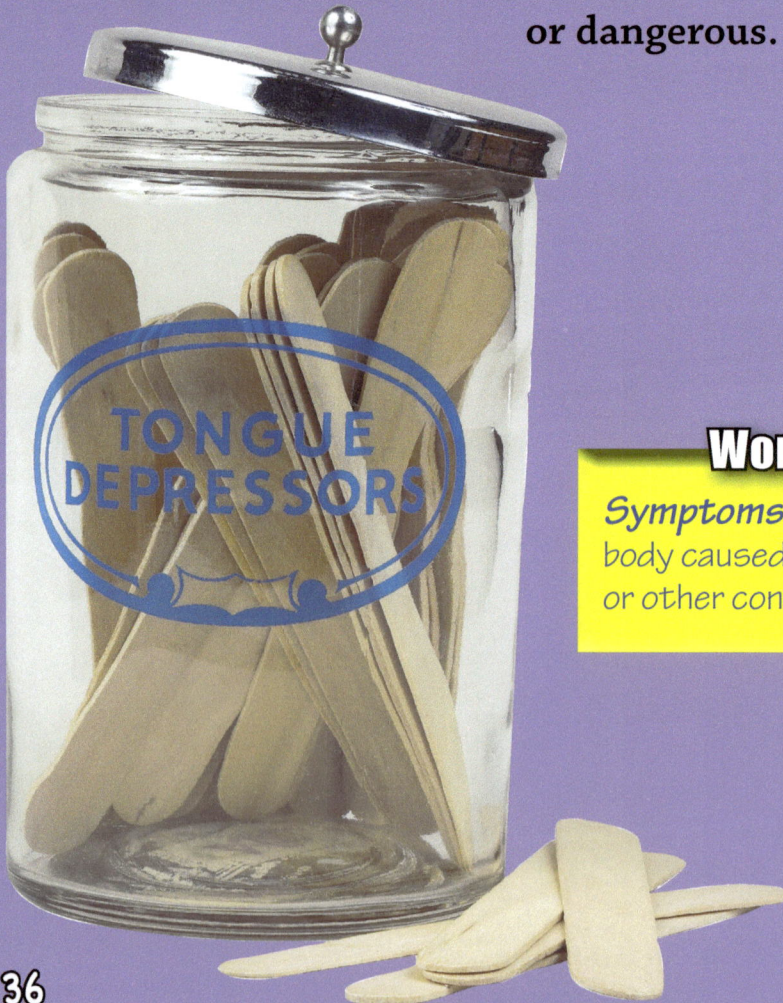

TONGUE DEPRESSORS

Words to Know

Symptoms: any changes in your body caused by a disease, allergy, or other condition.

Did You Know?

A normal temperature is 97 to 99.5 degrees Fahrenheit or 36.1 to 37.5 degrees Celsius. If your temperature is higher than that, it means you have a fever and your body is working to fight off an infection.

When you go to the doctor, expect that he or she will listen to your heart and lungs, look into your eyes and ears, take your temperature, and feel your stomach and throat for sore areas. Tell your doctor about anything that hurts or is uncomfortable.

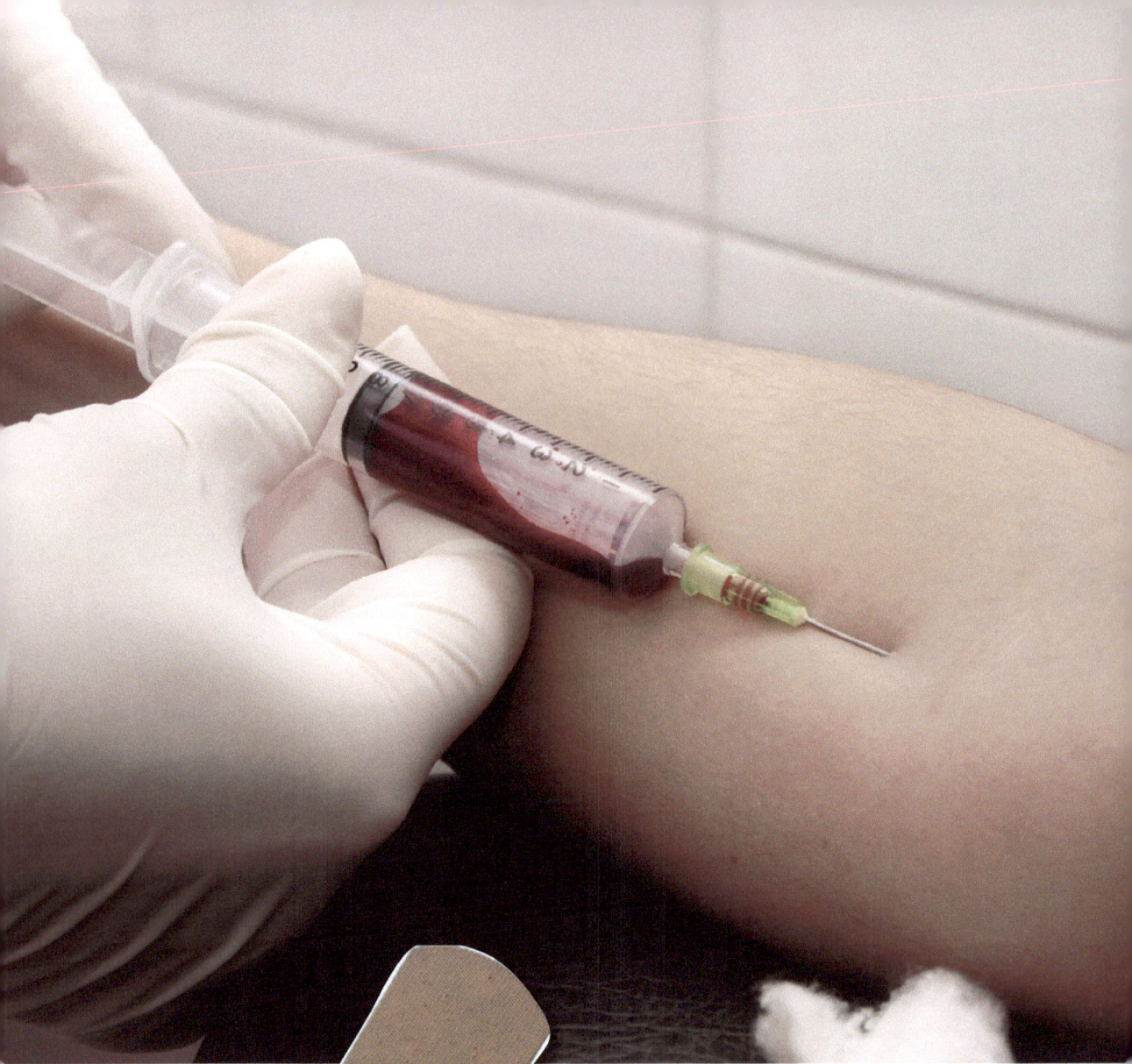

The doctor may also take a little bit of blood from your finger or arm. This hurts a little—but it only lasts a second.

When doctors look at your blood with a microscope, they can see if the tiny cells inside your blood (shown here) are normal. If they're not, this can tell the doctor you have a certain disease or condition. When the doctor or *lab* assistant looks at the blood, she may also see tiny parasites that don't belong there that may cause a certain disease. Other blood tests can tell doctors if bacteria or viruses are in your body.

Once your doctor knows what is wrong with you, he can begin to give you the medicine and other treatments that will help you feel better.

Words to Know

Lab: short for "laboratory," where scientific tests and procedures are performed.

Staying Safe

One way you can protect yourself against most bugs is by using repellent. Remember, though, that repellents contain chemicals that may be dangerous to humans (as well as bugs). Be careful not to get insect repellents in your eyes, mouth, or an open sore. Always spray away from food and flame. A chemical called DEET is the repellent that works best, but it also contains the strongest chemicals. Only use it when necessary. Wash it off your skin once you are no longer around bugs.

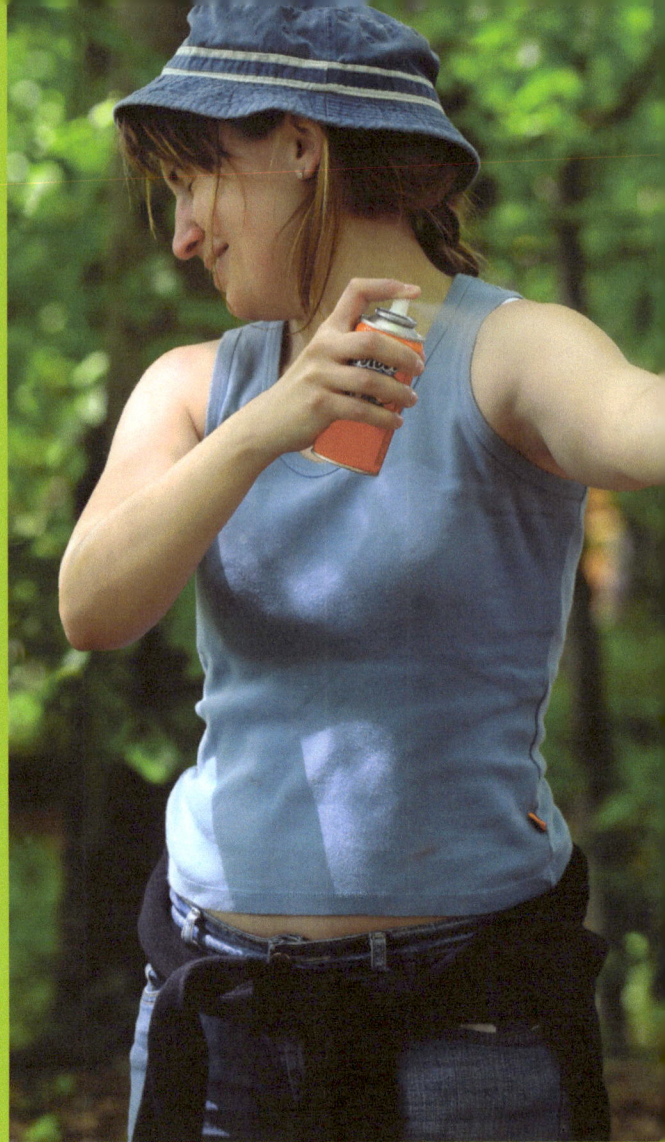

Did You Know?

Researchers have found that some plant-based alternatives to DEET work as well as low levels of DEET. However, they have to be put on your skin more often. Natural repellent, like all repellents, should not be used on very young children, as they can irritate sensitive skin.

One of the best and easiest ways to protect yourself from bug bites and stings is to simply cover up! When walking in wooded areas and tall grass, wear long sleeves, hats, and long pants.

I heard that kids are in the most danger of getting really sick from mosquito bites. Is that true?

A: No, it's not true. Although very young children may have more severe reactions because their bodies are so small, older kids are not at increased risk. In fact some insect-borne diseases, like West Nile virus, are much more apt to infect older adults than they are children.

Since many bugs breed in moist areas, one way to reduce the number of bugs is by reducing the number of places where they can breed. You can't drain all the swamps in your region (and it wouldn't be good for the environment if you could!), but you can remove empty barrels, buckets, old tires, and other places where water collects. Places like these are egg-laying sites for mosquitoes and other insects. Mowing the lawn often also reduces the number of bugs, as does keeping swimming pools *chlorinated* and keeping fish (that eat insect larvae) in ornamental pools.

Words to Know

Chlorinated: water that has a little bleach added to it to kill germs.

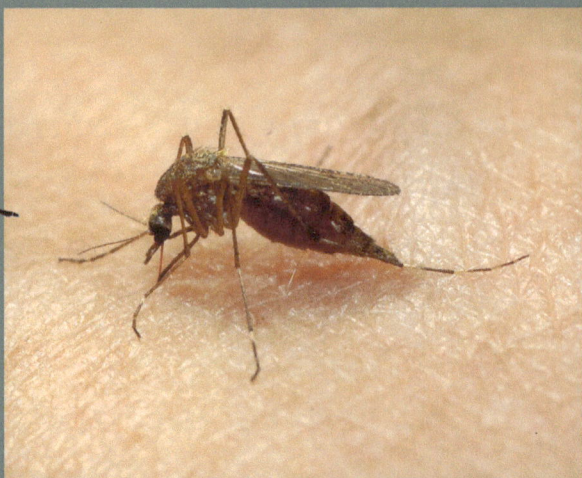

Mosquitoes are most active and likely to bite in the early evening and early morning. If you are outdoors during these times, wear socks and shoes with light-colored, long-sleeved shirts and pants that have fabric thick enough to keep mosquitoes from biting.

Citronella candles and mosquito coils can also help keep mosquitoes away from your picnic or deck. Electric devices—bug zappers—actually attract bugs, so they need to be placed away from where people linger.

Words to Know

Citronella: the oil from a kind of grass that has been found to repel insects.

If you use repellents that contain DEET, different concentrations will work better for different amounts of time.

30 percent DEET will work for about five hours.

10 percent DEET will give you about three hours of protection.

5 percent DEET give about two hours of protection.

If you live in or are visiting a region where mosquitoes are plentiful, mosquito netting over your bed gives you extra protection against these whiny (and sometimes dangerous) pests.

45

What the World Is Doing

Bugs are everywhere on our planet. Most of the time that's a good thing—but when bugs make people sick, it means that the problems they cause are worldwide. Insects don't respect nations' boundary lines. They just crawl, creep, and fly right on past! Sometimes they are carried from one part of the world to another when they are in ships or hidden inside goods that are *exported* from one country to another.

Words to Know

Exported: shipped to another region for sale or trade.

This means the people of the whole world need to work together to solve the problems that bugs cause. The United Nations is an international organization that works on lots of world problems—including bugs.

Did You Know?

The United Nations (UN) came into being in 1945. Since then, it has worked to protect the safety, health, and rights of all humans. The UN's New York City headquarters is shown to the left.

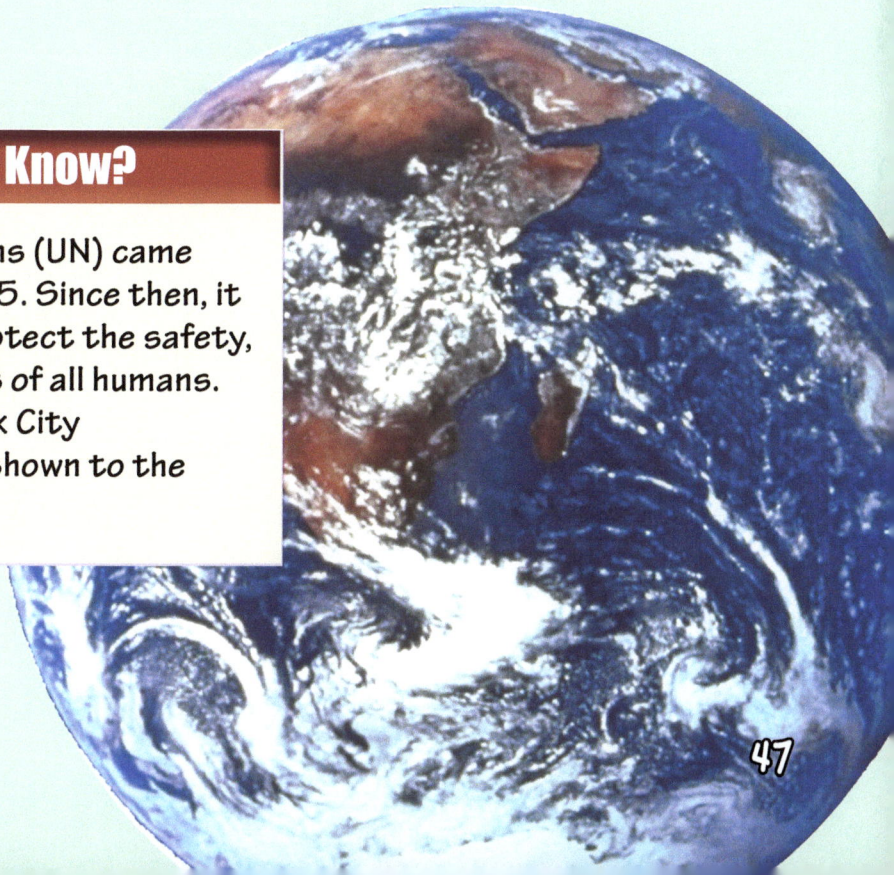

Being healthy is a basic human right. But it's a right that not every human being has. In many places of the world, there are too few doctors and medical facilities to treat diseases. Children may not be able to go to school, which means they will often not learn ways to keep themselves healthy, including how to protect themselves from bugs that can make them sick.

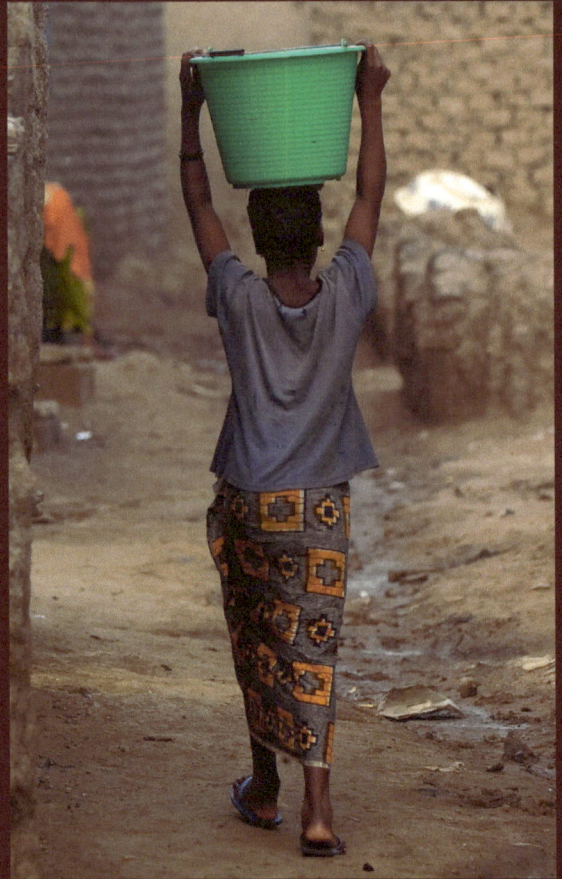

Poverty is a big problem that makes health problems even worse. Poverty is a bigger problem in certain parts of the world—for instance, Africa—but poverty is everywhere, in all parts of the globe. Poverty ties into many other problems that affect health. Poor communities, for example, may not have clean drinking water. They may not have *sanitation facilities*.

Words to Know

Poverty: not having enough of what you need to live.

Sanitation facilities: systems for dealing with garbage and human waste materials.

This means that the insects and other tiny creatures that cause disease may live in the water people drink and use for cooking and washing.

The United Nations is working to fight poverty, and improve the health of all people. The governments around the world are also doing their part. So are many charities and other organizations.

This work takes money—but children around the world deserve to be safe from the diseases bugs carry!

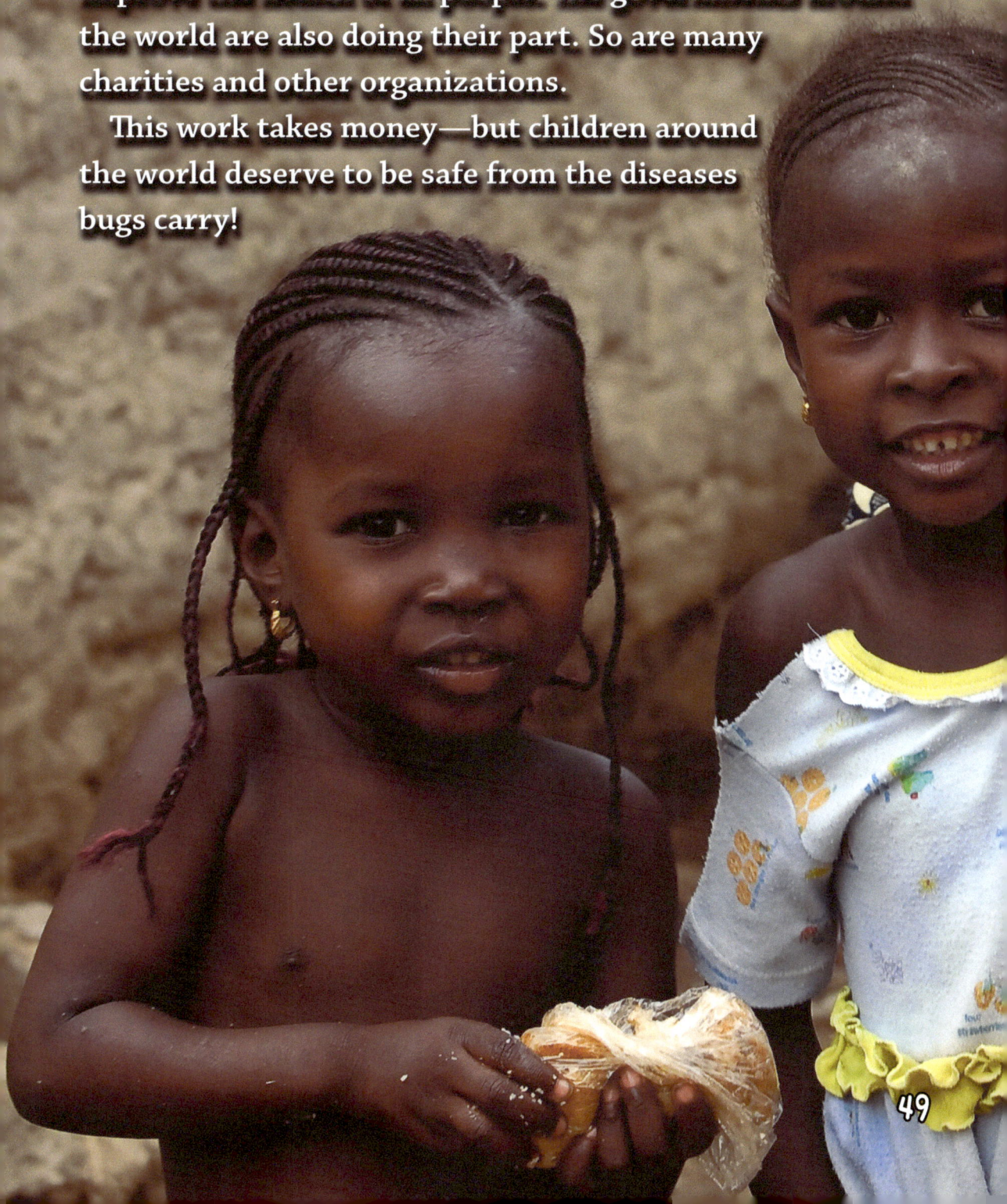

Research

One of the big ways that people around the world fight the diseases caused by bugs is by doing research.

Research means that scientists look very closely at a disease to find out what causes it, what can be done to prevent it, and what can be done to cure people who get it. Researchers look at both the big picture—and the very small picture. Both are important to understanding what causes a particular disease. So scientists may use microscopes to look closely at blood cells (shown here), or they may look at entire *communities* and count how many people have a particular disease or keep records of what other things are going on in that region.

Words to Know

Communities: groups of people living together, sharing certain things in common. A community can be small, such as a town or neighborhood—or it can be an entire planet.

Scientists believe that global warming may be increasing the number of cases of diseases caused by bugs. This is because pollution in our atmosphere is making our planet's average temperatures rise a little each year—and this in turn means that insects who need warm conditions to *breed* now have longer breeding seasons. It also means that these insects are spreading to regions of the world that were once too cold for them to live. As these insects' numbers increase, so do the diseases they cause.

Words to Know

Breed: to produce offspring, to give birth or hatch.

52

Interwoven: woven together, connected.

To better understand bugs, researchers take a close look at the places where bugs live. They bring samples back to their labs, where they look at them even more closely, or perform experiments that will increase their understanding of the ways bugs reproduce, how they spread disease, and what can be done to control their harmful effects on human beings.

Researchers can't just kill all bugs. If they did, they would hurt the rest of the environment (including human beings). Our environment is like a web of *interwoven* threads. You can't pull out one thread without changing all the others. This means researchers have to look at all the ways possible solutions could change other parts of our world.

MALARIA RESEARCH

Scientists have sometimes built on old ideas to find new and better treatments for the diseases carried by bugs.

For example, recently researchers found that a Chinese herbal drug called sweet wormwood (which has been used to treat malaria and other fevers for thousands of years) contains a chemical that can be used to make a stronger and quicker cure for malaria. Even better, this medicine is safer because it has fewer *side effects*. However, it is still too expensive for use in many of the world's poorest countries.

Did You Know?

An antibody is a Y-shaped protein (illustrated in the image to the right) made by white blood cells to fight off "bad" things that get in the blood (like a virus, bacteria, or parasite). Each antibody can only attach itself to a specific kind of enemy, so once you have antibodies for a particular disease, your body is better able to fight off that sickness.

WEST NILE VIRUS RESEARCH

Researchers also noticed that some people get milder forms of West Nile virus, so scientists developed an antibody like the ones in the blood of people who are able to fight off the disease. This man-made antibody may eventually provide an effective treatment for West Nile.

DUST MITE RESEARCH

Researchers have found that when people who have damaged lungs are exposed to mite droppings, their allergies to other substances also become worse. Mite *allergens* poke a hole in the lungs' defense system that then allows harmful bacteria and fungus into the lungs. Scientists now believe that this may be why people with asthma develop more lung infections than healthy people.

Words to Know

Allergens: substances that trigger allergies (sensitivities).

Did You Know?

Although the house dust mite lives for only three months, as a species it has been on the Earth for over 23 million years.

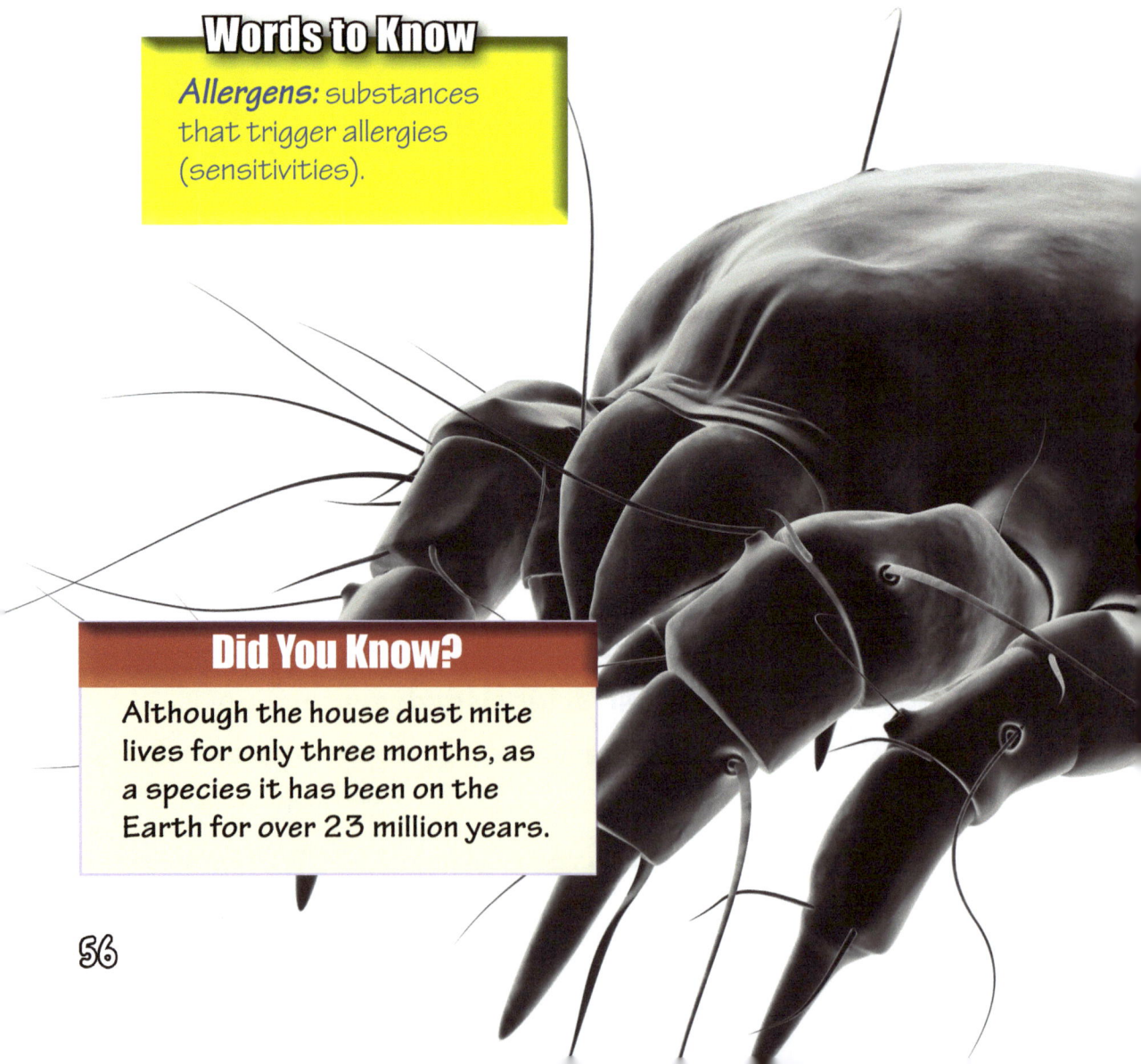

LYME DISEASE RESEARCH

The United States now has a vaccine that helps prevent Lyme disease. It's approved for use in people fifteen to seventy years of age who live or work in grassy or wooded areas where infected ticks live. Although the vaccine protects most people, it won't prevent all cases of Lyme disease—so people still need to wear protective clothing and use tick repellent.

Real Kids

Isabella is eleven years old. She lives in Kenya. And she has had bouts of malaria ever since she was a baby.

This means that she often gets sick with high fevers and muscle *convulsions*. Sometimes she will be playing, feeling perfectly fine, when she notices her stomach and head hurt. Wiithin a few hours, she will be sick in bed. Her mother worries about her all the time, so it's hard for Isabella to feel like a normal child. She is not allowed to sleep at a friend's house or be away from her mother for more than a few hours.

Words to Know

Convulsions: when muscles contract uncontrollably and involuntarily.

"I have to go in the hospital every few weeks," Isabella said. "I hate it. I wish someone would make a medicine that would make me better forever." In the hospital, Isabella receives quinine, the only medicine that is available to her in her community.

"But I think I'm lucky," Isabella told a nurse at the hospital. "I know people who died from malaria or who are sicker than me. I get tired of being sick so often, but at least I'm still alive."

Did You Know?

Lyme disease received its name in 1975 after a mysterious outbreak of what people thought was arthritis in children who lived near Lyme, Connecticut. The children felt tired, stiff, and achy. Scientists believe, however, that Lyme disease has been around for a long time, even though doctors didn't know what was causing it.

Find Out More

American Academy of Allergy, Asthma, & Immunology: Just for Kids
www.aaaai.org/conditions-and-treatments/just-for-kids.aspx

Asthma and Allergies
kids.niehs.nih.gov/explore/pollute/asthma_and_allergies.htm

Dust Mites and Allergies
www.cellsalive.com/mite.htm

Dust Mites: Everything You Might Not Want to Know!
www.ehso.com/ehshome/dustmites.php

Lyme Disease
www.kidshealth.org/kid/ ill_injure/sick/lyme_disease.html

Malaria No More
www.malarianomore.org/malaria

What's West Nile Virus?
kidshealth.org/kid/ill_injure/aches/west_nile.html

World Health Organization: Malaria
www.who.int/topics/malaria/en

Index

Picture Credits

Dreamstime
Alien Cat & Michael
Adcock: p. 21
Allyn, Dawn: p 29
Bernardo: p. 48-49
Big I Design: pp. 62–63
Bruce, Leo: p. 46
Cammeraydave: p. 61
Cribeiro: p. 26
Davisales: p. 63
Ecophoto: p. 28
Eraxion: p. 13,34, 55
The Final Miracle: p. 24
Gregor: pp. 10–11
JivDream: p. 57
Kgtoh: p. 45
Mailthepic: p. 61
Thomasdian: p. 3
New Photo Service: p. 54
Orla: p. 22

Pailoolom: p. 16
PhotoEuphoria: p. 37
Photoka: p. 8
Photowitch: p. 57
Rocher: p. 33
Rolffimages: pp. 50–51
Shariff: p. 9
iStockphotos:
pp. 27, 38, 42
Bowker, Martin: p. 43
Hillman, Robert
    Adrian: p. 44
Warren, Sean: p. 49
Purdue University: p. 20
U.S. Centers for
    Disease Control:
    pp. 14,15,17
Vermaat, David: p. 12
Vermaat, Peter: p. 12

To the best knowledge of the publisher, all other images are in the public domain. If any image has been inadvertently uncredited, please notify Village Earth Press, Vestal, New York 13850, so that rectification can be made for future printings.

About the Author

Rae Simons has written many books for young adults and children. She lives in upstate New York with her family.

About the Consultant

Elise DeVore Berlan, MD, MPH, FAAP, is a faculty member of the Division of Adolescent Health at Nationwide Children's Hospital and an Assistant Professor of Clinical Pediatrics at the Ohio State University College of Medicine. She completed her fellowship in adolescent medicine at Children's Hospital Boston and obtained a master's degree in public health at the Harvard School of Public Health. Dr. Berlan completed her residency in pediatrics at the Children's Hospital of Philadelphia, where she also served an additional year as chief resident. She received her medical degree from the University of Iowa College of Medicine.

www.ingramcontent.com/pod-product-compliance
Lightning Source LLC
Chambersburg PA
CBHW042017080426
42735CB00002B/81